Hors d'Oeuvres and Appetizers

Mimi Sheraton

Hors d'Oeuvres & Appetizers

With Illustrations by
Walter Swartz

HALLMARK EDITIONS

CONTENTS

...From Antipasto to Zakouskis

Every nation has its favorite array of appetizers, from the *antipasto* of Italy and the *entremeses* of South America to the *Zakouskis* of Russia and Baltic Europe. In Germany the word is *Vorspeisen* and throughout the Middle East it is *Meze*, but by any name, the implication of the course is the same. It is food taken before the meal, or, in a direct translation of the French *hors d'oeuvres*, it is "outside the main work," namely the meal. Appetizers are meant to whet the appetite but not to satisfy it and that is the clue that should guide you in your planning. You will want them to be tempting and piquant, light and not too filling. They are foods that make you want more food.

No other course, save dessert, offers the hostess as much chance to display her culinary ingenuity as this one does. Hors d'oeuvres must tempt the eye as well as the palate and so should be presented attractively and should vary in color, texture, form and flavor. Garnishes should be colorful but simple and it is best if they are related to the food being served. Such standards as radish roses, carrot curls, flowerets of cauliflower and broccoli, quartered hard-cooked eggs and sprigs of parsley, cress and dill, are much more valid than inedible flowers, leaves and the like. The following are just a few simple touches you might want to consider for your next hors d'oeuvres tray, ending with one that never fails to make me laugh when I come across it in Germany—the *Fliegenpilz*, or fly-specked mushroom that has a whimsical Hansel and Gretel touch to it.

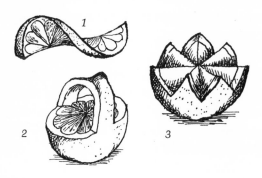

1. *Butterfly curl of lemon—Cut lemon slice almost in half, but leave one side of rind uncut. Twist into curl as shown and set on top of fish canapes and salads.*
2. *Lemon basket which can be hollowed out to hold mustard, mayonnaise or horseradish.*
3. *Another fancy lemon cut which looks especially nice on fish platters.*

6

4. Sweet gherkins or pickled cornichons can be sliced and fanned out this way. Place on top of canapes or alongside hors d'oeuvres.

5. Variations of the radish rose theme.

6. Pimento stuffed olives are colorful stand-bys.

7. Spears of white or green asparagus tips, held by a pimento "ribbon."

8. Fliegenpilz—Cut hard-cooked egg in half and trim off pointed tip. Top with half of small tomato. Dice leftover egg white, dip into mayonnaise and dot over tomato cap to make "flies."

Quick appetizers from pantry and freezer

Smoked oysters and mussels: Serve with lemon juice, or, wrap in slices of bacon and broil.

Tuna Fish: For dips and spreads, or, serve in chunks with White Beans Vinaigrette.

Canned White Beans (Cannelini): Serve with Vinaigrette Sauce, or, as above.

Anchovies: Serve on buttered toast, or, use to flavor other appetizers.

Capers and Olives: Hors d'oeuvre essentials.

Italian Roasted Peppers: Serve with anchovies and capers, or, as garnish.

Canned meat spreads: For canapes and dips, or, as fillings for celery and cherry tomatoes.

Artichoke Hearts: Frozen or canned: Serve with Vinaigrette Sauce, or, fold into thick cream sauce, sprinkle with grated cheese and brown under broiler.

Canned Salami and Ham: Serve with curls of butter, or, folded into Cornucopias, Page 12.

Egg Rolls, Ravioli, Won-ton (Frozen): Deep fry for crisp hors d'oeuvres tidbits that can be dipped into mustard, barbecue, or pizza sauce.

Escargots: French snails in cans, packed with shells and instructions for sauce, make excellent last minute appetizers for sit-down dinners.

I
Please Pass the Hors d'Oeuvres

Cold Appetizers

9

Smoked salmon, sturgeon, whitefish, eel and trout, are about the simplest and most elegant appetizers—barring caviar—that you can serve. Nova Scotia salmon and sturgeon are readily available at fine gourmet food shops and delicatessens, and are sliced for you so that you need only arrange them with their garnishes. Filets of smoked eel and trout may be a little harder to find, unless you live in a fairly large city, but they are worth looking for when you want a special touch to a dinner party.

All of these fish are best without lettuce or any other salad garnish. Arrange them on salad or dinner plates, surrounded with trimmings such as drained capers, lemons cut in wedges or paper-thin slices, and triangles of buttered Westphalian pumpernickel. You can add minced hard-cooked egg whites and yolk (separately) and minced onion also if you like. Horseradish cream, prepared according to the recipe below, is a wonderful touch with these fish.

Simple canapes can be made with any smoked fish. Just arrange in thin slices on pieces of buttered Westphalian pumpernickel and top with lemon, or horseradish cream and capers.

HORSERADISH CREAM

About 1 cup

1 cup heavy sweet cream
1 tablespoon lemon juice
Pinch of salt
2 teaspoons sugar
½ horseradish root, peeled and grated

Whip cream and as it begins to thicken, add lemon juice, salt and sugar. When mixture is the consistency of heavy sour cream, fold in grated horseradish. Chill until serving time. If you cannot get fresh horseradish root, substitute 2 tablespoons, drained bottled horseradish and eliminate the lemon juice. A little minced, peeled apple can also be added to this sauce.

SMOKED SALMON CORNUCOPIAS

12 to 25 servings

15 slices smoked salmon
2 cups red caviar
10 thin slices of lemon, cut in quarters
Sour cream (optional) or dill (optional)

Form the pieces of salmon into cornucopias and secure with toothpick, or merely press them closed for a second or two and they should hold. Fill each with a dab of red caviar and stick a little piece of lemon, rind and all, in the opening. A tiny dab of sour cream could be added if you like, or a small spray of fresh dill. Although 45 such cornucopias sound like a lot, they are quite small and some guests will take two.

VARIATIONS: Other foods which lend themselves to this treatment are slices of sturgeon, ham, salami and baloney. Fill with mixtures such as cream cheese flavored with chives, olives, pimento, or walnuts, the Vegetable Salad, Page 20, chopped egg salad, flavored mayonnaise or Tapenade, Page 46. Sprigs of cress add touches of color. Horseradish Cream is an excellent filling for Smoked Salmon Cornucopias.

MEAT SALAD PIQUANTE

6 to 8 servings
3 cups diced, cold, cooked beef, ham or tongue
2 dill pickles, diced
1 medium-sized onion, sliced
1 tablespoon capers
1 tablespoon minced parsley
1 teaspoon prepared mustard
2 medium-sized boiled potatoes, diced
Salt and pepper to taste

MARINADE:
3 tablespoons olive oil
3 tablespoons vinegar
3 tablespoons cold beef stock

Mix marinade well. Toss all other ingredients together and pour marinade over them. Mix thoroughly, season to taste. Chill 2 hours and garnish with hard-cooked egg slices. This appetizer makes excellent use of leftover meats.

VIENNESE CRABMEAT COCKTAIL

4 servings

1 pound cooked fresh crabmeat
¼ cup catsup
1 cup whipped cream
1 tablespoon drained, canned crushed pineapple
1 small apple, peeled and diced
4 tablespoons cognac
Few drops Worcestershire sauce

Pick over crabmeat and remove all spiny fragments. Fold catsup into whipped cream and stir in cognac and Worcestershire sauce. Fold in crabmeat, pineapple and apple and pile into sherbet glasses lined with a lettuce leaf.

STUFFED CUCUMBER SLICES

1 large or 2 small cucumbers
½ pound cream cheese
1 tablespoon minced chives

Wash cucumbers but do not peel. Instead, make ridges down the sides with the tines of a fork. Cut off ends. If cucumber is very long, cut in half. Using an apple corer, scrape out center of cucumbers.

Mash cream cheese until smooth, mixing in chives. If cheese seems very stiff, thin slightly with a little sweet or sour cream, but mixture should be fairly stiff. Pack cream cheese into hollowed cucumber. Wrap in wax paper and chill. Cut in thin slices just before serving.

WHITE BEANS VINAIGRETTE

3 cups

2 cans cooked white kidney beans
½ cup olive oil
¼ cup lemon juice
Salt and pepper
½ teaspoon dry mustard
Chopped parsley and chives
1 clove garlic, whole

Empty beans into a large colander and rinse once or twice. Drain well, place in a bowl and toss in olive oil, lemon juice, salt, pepper, and mustard, so that beans are evenly coated. Adjust quantities so flavor is neither too oily nor too sour. Leave in serving bowl and add garlic, burying it in the mixture. Chill for 1 hour. Remove garlic, turn beans into serving dishes and sprinkle on a mixture of chopped chives and parsley.

EIGHT WAYS TO DEVIL AN EGG

BASIC RECIPE:
6 hard-cooked eggs, shelled
2 tablespoons mayonnaise
1 teaspoon prepared mustard
Salt and white pepper, to taste
Paprika or capers for garnish

Peel eggs under running cold water and dry. Cut in half, lengthwise, and remove yolks. Mash with a fork and blend in mayonnaise, mustard, salt and pepper. Adjust seasoning and consistency to suit yourself. Spoon filling back into whites, heaping it fairly high. (Use a spoon or force yolk mixture through a pastry tube, swirling it as you do so.) Chill until serving time. Top with paprika or capers just before serving.

VARIATIONS ALL BASED ON 6 EGGS:

1. Add 1 teaspoon anchovy paste or 3 mashed anchovy filets to yolks. Garnish with capers.

2. Mash yolks with 2 thin slices smoked salmon, 2 tablespoons sour cream, 1 teaspoon grated onion and pepper to taste. Garnish with a dab of red or black caviar.

3. Mash yolks with 2 teaspoons red or black caviar, 1 tablespoon sour cream and a dash of

lemon juice. Garnish with chives.

4. Follow basic recipe, adding 1 tablespoon canned ham or tongue spread to yolk mixture. A pinch of curry powder can be added to mayonnaise. Garnish with a slice of gherkin.

5. Mash yolks with 2 teaspoons crumbled Roquefort or Bleu cheese and 2 tablespoons sour cream. Garnish with minced chives or olive.

6. Follow basic recipe, omit mustard and add 1 tablespoon minced fresh green herbs such as parsley, chives, dill, chervil, tarragon—either alone or in combination, but the total amount should not be more than 1 tablespoonful.

7. Mash egg yolks with 1 tablespoon grated cheddar cheese, a dab of mustard and 2 tablespoons sour cream. Sprinkle tops with crumbled, crisp bacon.

See also Tapenade, Page 46.

SWEDISH HERRING IN MUSTARD DILL SAUCE

2½ cups

For best results, use the Swedish herring known as *gaffelbittar*, or any other bottled maatjes herring pieces packed in wine or dill sauce. Do not use herring packed in cream.

2 cups herring tidbits
⅓ to ½ cup hot yellow prepared mustard
⅓ to ½ cup sweet brown prepared mustard
2 to 3 tablespoons olive oil
2 to 3 tablespoons distilled vinegar
2 generous tablespoons minced fresh dill
Sugar, to taste

Rinse herring tidbits for a second or two under running cold water and drain. Reserve jars in which herring was packed. Combine the two mustards with enough olive oil and vinegar, added alternately, to give you a smooth, fairly thick consistency. Add herring and dill and stir in gently. Correct seasoning with sugar, as needed. Return to jars and chill for several hours before serving.

POACHED EGGS IN MADRILENE ASPIC

6 servings

6 eggs
1 can madrilene
6 sprays of tarragon
1½ envelopes plain gelatin
3 tablespoons white vinegar
6 slices pate de foie gras *or good liverwurst*

Poach eggs in water which has vinegar added to it. Time them so whites are set but yolks are soft. Remove with slotted spoon, put on plate, cool and trim whites into perfect rounds. Put unjelled madrilene into saucepan and combine with gelatin. Heat slowly to boiling point. Cool, but do not let it set—if it does, reheat it until melted. Spoon a thin layer of madrilene into each of six round or oval ramekins and arrange tarragon sprays attractively over this layer. Slip one egg into each mold, and place a slice of pate on top. Fill the mold with the liquid aspic. Chill for 2 hours. To serve, wipe the outside of the molds with a cloth wrung out in hot water. Turn over onto serving dish or on bed of lettuce.

VEGETABLE SALAD WITH
TARRAGON MAYONNAISE

4 cups

1 cup diced canned baby carrots
1 cup tiny canned lima beans
1 cup canned green peas
1 cup canned string beans cut into 1" lengths
2 tablespoons lemon juice
½ teaspoon dried tarragon
Salt and black pepper
2 teaspoons minced fresh dill
3 to 4 tablespoons mayonnaise

Drain the vegetables well and place in earthen-ware or glass mixing bowl. Sprinkle with lemon juice, and add the seasonings and mayonnaise. Toss slightly with fork, and add more mayonnaise if the salad seems to need more binding, but do not add too much as the dressing should be light. Refrigerate until serving time.

MORTADELLA OR BALONEY PIE

2 pies

½ pound cream cheese (2 standard packages)
1 to 2 tablespoons sour cream
2 teaspoons prepared mustard
Few drops Worcestershire sauce
¼ cup minced chives
1 pound wide baloney or Italian mortadella,
*   not too thinly sliced*

Let cream cheese soften at room temperature for about 15 minutes. Mash and soften with a little sour cream, working in mustard and Worcestershire sauce until you have a smooth, creamy paste. Mix in chives.

Remove casing from meat slices. Try not to tear slices. Spread one side of each slice of meat with the cream cheese spread. Pile them up layer cake fashion so there is cheese between each two slices of meat. The top slice should not have any spread on it.

The amounts called for here will make two pies. Wrap each in wax paper, place on a plate and chill for at least 2 hours. Before serving, cut pies into wedges, reshape as pies and serve.

ARTICHOKE HEARTS, ARMENIAN STYLE

Sayat Nova, New York's best Armenian restaurant, is famous for this appetizer.

6 servings

6 very large artichokes
2 lemons
4 medium-sized onions
4 medium-sized potatoes
1 cup olive oil
1 tablespoon sugar
2½ cups water, or as needed
Salt and white pepper, to taste
1 tablespoon minced fresh dill

Break off outer 2 or 3 rows of artichoke leaves. Using a sharp knife, cut off remaining leaves right down to the base or heart. Scoop out choke (the fuzzy substance) and peel outer skin from stem and base. Keep rubbing artichoke surfaces with lemon as you cut, to prevent blackening. Drop each heart into a bowl of salted water as you finish it, and add lemon pieces to water.

Peel onions and cut in quarters. Peel potatoes and cut in slices ¼ to ½ inch thick. Cut artichoke hearts in half, lengthwise, through the stem. Place in enameled skillet, cut side down.

Fit onion and potato slices around hearts. Sprinkle with salt, white pepper, and dill. Add about ⅓ cup olive oil.

Cover artichokes with an inverted dinner plate. The plate should fit very snugly inside the rim of the skillet. Pour the water over the plate. If the plate does not fit tightly enough, the water will run into the skillet and the vegetables will boil instead of steaming. Cover pan with its lid.

Cook over medium heat for 1 hour. If water evaporates, add more. Add remaining olive oil to artichokes for the last 10 minutes of cooking time. Replace plate and lid; continue cooking.

Cool at room temperature. Artichokes look best when served with two halves together, stems up. Potatoes and onions are served with them, as is a wedge of fresh lemon.

BEEF TARTAR APPETIZER

For each serving

4 ounces lean beef (filet or sirloin) ground or,
*   preferably, scraped*
1 egg yolk
1 teaspoon olive oil
1 anchovy, chopped
1 teaspoon freshly ground horseradish
5 capers, chopped
Pinch each of salt, pepper and paprika
Dash of Worcestershire sauce
1 slice buttered toast, crusts removed
½ ounce fresh caviar (fresh-pressed would be
*   good here)*
1 tablespoon onion, minced

Grind or scrape beef just before preparing recipe. Mix beef, egg yolk, oil, anchovy, horseradish, capers, seasonings and Worcestershire sauce together thoroughly. Spread on buttered toast and top with caviar. Serve with minced onion on the side along with a sliced gherkin. Or, form tiny patties with meat mixture and set each on a square of thin rye bread or pumpernickel.

II
From the Buffet & Chafing Dish

Hot Appetizers

25

SESAME BAKED CLAMS

4 to 6 servings

24 fresh cherrystone clams on the half shell
¼ cup canned bean sprouts
6 whole, canned water chestnuts, drained
4 scallions, finely chopped
2 teaspoons soya sauce
½ teaspoon minced fresh ginger, or ¼ teaspoon
    powdered ginger
1 cup thick cream sauce
¼ cup grated Parmesan cheese
½ to ¾ cup sesame seeds
Rock salt, optional

Remove clams from shell (or have them removed at the market) but reserve shells. Drain clams thoroughly on paper toweling. Turn bean sprouts into a strainer and rinse under running cold water; drain well, pressing out excess water.

Mince clams and water chestnuts and combine with bean sprouts and chopped scallions. Season to taste with soya sauce and ginger. Combine with ⅓ cup cream sauce.

Spoon clam mixture onto half shells. Stir grated cheese into remaining hot cream sauce; spoon sauce over the top of each stuffed clam shell. Sprinkle with a layer of sesame seeds.

Fill a shallow baking pan with rock salt. Set stuffed clams on top of salt and bake in 450° oven for about 5 minutes. Serve right from baking dish, as salt will keep clams hot. If you cannot get rock salt, set clams in baking dish without it, but bake in 375° oven for 10-15 minutes instead and serve immediately.

BAKED OYSTERS TARANTINO

2 to 6 servings

12 fresh oysters on half shells
¾ cup bread crumbs
2 tablespoons grated Parmesan cheese
1 tablespoon grated lemon rind
½ cup butter, melted
Salt and pepper
2 tablespoons butter

Mix bread crumbs with grated cheese and lemon rind. Drain shelled oysters and dip each into melted butter. Sprinkle with salt and pepper. Roll each oyster in bread crumb mixture until well coated on all sides. Replace oysters on half shells. Arrange in shallow baking pan. Bake in 425° oven for about 10 minutes, or until oysters are crusty and golden. Serve with a little melted butter, cheese and lemon on the sides.

RIGATONI PRIMAVERA

6 to 8 servings

¾ pound rigatoni (short, wide, tubular
    macaroni)
1½ pounds spinach
3 tablespoons butter
¾ pound ricotta cheese
1 egg
¼ pound Parmesan cheese, grated
Dash of nutmeg
Salt, to taste
3 tablespoons butter
2½ tablespoons flour
2 to 2½ cups milk

Cook rigatoni in boiling salted water 10 to 12 minutes, or until tender.

While macaroni cooks, wash spinach well and cook until tender (about 5 minutes), using only the water that clings to the leaves from washing. Drain well in colander, pressing out excess water. Put spinach in towel and twist to squeeze out remaining water. Puree through a sieve or in a food mill. Add 3 tablespoons butter to spinach and simmer, covered, for a minute or two to "season."

Mash ricotta cheese with spinach, add egg and

half of grated cheese. Season with nutmeg and salt. Beat with wooden spoon until very smooth.

Drain cooked rigatoni in a colander and run a little cold water over it so it becomes cool enough to handle. Drain thoroughly. Using a pastry tube or a small teaspoon, fill each rigatoni with some of the spinach mixture.

Make a medium thick cream sauce with the butter, flour and milk. Beat with a wire whisk so it becomes very smooth.

Spoon a layer of sauce on bottom of baking pan (use a 12" round, or, an 11" x 8" rectangle, each 2½" to 3" deep). Add one layer of macaroni, another of sauce and keep alternating in that way until pan is full. Finish with a layer of sauce. Sprinkle with remaining grated cheese and dot with butter. Bake in 350° oven for 30 minutes, or until top is golden brown and sauce is bubbling.

HOT CRABMEAT PUFFS

About 3 dozen puffs

CREAM PUFF PASTRY:
½ cup water
¼ cup butter
Pinch of salt
Pinch of sugar
½ cup flour
2 small eggs

Put water and butter in a 1-quart saucepan and simmer over low heat until butter melts and water comes to a boil. Lower heat and add salt, sugar and flour, all at once. Stir briskly and constantly over low heat for 4 or 5 minutes, until mixture forms a ball and leaves sides of the pan.

Remove from heat. Add one egg, beating it in completely. Beat the second egg and add it gradually until the mixture is stiff enough to form a peak when the spoon is pulled out of it.

Shape tiny puffs either by dropping a scant teaspoonful of batter onto a lightly buttered baking sheet, or by forcing it through the number 7 tube of a pastry bag, in small, high mounds. Bake in 375° oven for 25 to 30 minutes, or until puffs are golden brown and completely dry. Stick the point of a paring knife into the side of each puff. Turn off oven but leave puffs inside to dry for 10 minutes. If you do not dry them, the puffs may collapse.

Split puffs into halves crosswise and spoon in the following filling:

1½ cups cooked crab meat
⅓ cup chopped mushrooms
Salt
1 tablespoon butter
Tabasco sauce
1 tablespoon cream, if necessary

Put crabmeat through the fine blade of a food grinder twice. Saute chopped mushrooms in butter until dry and faintly golden and add to crabmeat. Season with salt and a dash or two of Tabasco sauce, and if the mixture seems very crumbly, moisten to a paste with a little cream. Mix thoroughly and spoon into puffs.

VARIATIONS: Lobster, shrimp, tuna fish, minced smoked salmon with scrambled eggs and chives, chopped chicken livers, ham or tongue spread, whipped cream cheese with chives or caviar are other fillings that work well in these puffs.

PIROSHKI

Paula Peck's Cream Cheese Pastry:
1 cup cream cheese
1 cup butter
¼ cup heavy cream
2½ cups flour
1 teaspoon salt

Let butter and cream cheese soften at room temperature for 10 minutes. Cream together and when well blended, work in cream. Add flour and salt a little at a time until smoothly blended. Shape dough into a ball, wrap in wax paper and chill 4 or 5 hours.

Roll dough between sheets of wax paper; lift paper every two or three rolls, so dough can spread. Cut into rectangles, about 2″ x 3″. Spoon filling onto center of each piece, roll and pinch closed. Arrange on a baking sheet and chill until baking time. Bake in 350° oven 10 to 15 minutes or until golden brown.

FILLING: Saute 1 small minced onion in 2 tablespoons butter until soft and yellow. Add 1 tablespoon minced chives and 2 cups coarsely ground cooked meat or poultry. Add 1 or 2 eggs, to make a thick pasty mixture. Season to taste.

SAUCISSON EN CROUTE

About 6 servings

1 coarsely ground French garlic sausage, or,
1 Italian coteghino sausage, ¾ to 1 pound
1 recipe Paula Peck's Cream Cheese Pastry,
(preceding recipe)

You will need a pot that will hold sausage without making it necessary to bend or break it. Poach sausage in water to cover for 1 hour. Keep water simmering steadily, but do not let it come to a rapid boil or sausage might burst. Do not pierce sausage casing at any time during the cooking. Remove sausage from water, drain and cool. Remove casing very carefully. Cool completely before rolling in dough.

Roll pastry out between sheets of waxed paper, as described. Roll it into a rectangular shape, about ¼ inch thick. When sausage has cooled, wrap it in dough. Pinch edges and end openings closed. Chill for 1 hour in refrigerator.

Set on a baking sheet, not in a pan with sides. Bake in 350° oven for 10 to 14 minutes, or until pastry is golden brown and crisp.

Using a sharp knife, cut in slices, ½ to ¾ inch thick. Serve hot with Dijon mustard and warm French potato salad with vinaigrette dressing.

SPIEDINI OF MOZZARELLA WITH ANCHOVY CAPER SAUCE

4 to 6 servings

1 long loaf of French or Italian bread
1 cup half-and-half (milk and cream)
1½ pounds mozzarella cheese
1 cup flour
2 eggs
4 tablespoons butter
5 tablespoons olive oil
Six 8-inch metal skewers

Sauce:
½ cup butter
1 small can anchovy filets, minced
2 tablespoons capers, drained and chopped
Lemon juice
2 tablespoons minced parsley

Cut the bread into slices about ½ to ¾ inch thick, and trim off crusts. Sprinkle the bread slices on both sides with milk so that they are moistened but not too soggy to handle. Cut mozzarella in slices that are the same size and thickness as the bread. Thread alternate slices of cheese and bread onto each skewer, beginning and ending with bread. You should have about 6 pieces of bread and 5 pieces of cheese on each. Keep slices close together.

Turn flour onto a large piece of waxed paper. Beat eggs lightly in a wide flat bowl, adding 1 tablespoon of cold water as you do so. Dip each skewer of bread and cheese into flour, coating all sides, then into egg, letting excess drip off. Roll again in flour. Be sure all sides are well coated. Heat butter and oil in a very large skillet and fry the spiedini slowly, turning frequently so they become golden brown on all sides. Serve on skewers, sliding the bread and cheese off on to a dinner plate.

The following sauce can be made while the spiedini fry, and should be served very hot on the side: melt butter in a small skillet and in it saute the minced anchovies for a minute or two. Add drained, chopped capers, a dash or two of lemon juice and the minced parsley. Heat for a few seconds, serve in heated sauce bowl and spoon over spiedini after they are on plates.

CURRIED LOBSTER QUICHE

2 to 4 servings

PASTRY:

1 cup flour
Pinch each, salt and sugar
5 tablespoons butter
1½ tablespoons chilled vegetable shortening
3 tablespoons cold water
2 cups dried beans

FILLING:

3 eggs
1½ cups heavy sweet cream
1 tablespoon melted butter
½ teaspoon salt
Dash of cayenne pepper
½ teaspoon curry powder
1 cup cooked lobster meat, coarsely chopped

To make pastry: Sift flour, sugar and salt together into a chilled earthenware or metal mixing bowl. Cut the butter and shortening into the flour using two knives, a pastry blender or your fingertips. Work quickly so shortening does not melt. Mixture should not look greasy. Cut fat in until dough is the texture of coarse meal.

Add cold water and quickly blend into dough

until you can gather it into a ball. If mixture is too flaky, add a little more cold water very slowly, but not more than an additional tablespoon should be necessary. Press into a ball, place on a lightly floured board and knead with heel of hand for 2 minutes. Reshape dough into ball, cover with wax paper and chill for 1 hour. Roll it into a flat circle between two sheets of waxed paper. Lift paper several times during rolling to allow dough to expand. Dough should be between ⅛ and ¼ inch thick. Set it loosely into an 8-inch round layer cake pan. Trim and crimp the edges. Fit a piece of foil into pan, covering dough. Fill pan with dried beans to keep dough from buckling. Bake in 400° oven for 10 minutes, or until pastry is firm.

Remove beans and foil, prick bottom dough with fork and bake for another 3 or 4 minutes. Cool. Tap pan gently and ease the shell out. Place on a cake rack until you are ready to fill.

To make filling: Beat eggs, cream, melted butter and seasonings in a bowl until thoroughly mixed. Add lobster meat and stir through. Check seasonings and correct.

Set pie shell on baking sheet and fill. Preheat oven to 375° and bake for 30 minutes, or until custard is set and brown on top.

COCONUT SHRIMP LUAU

About 20 shrimps, or 10 servings
2 pounds raw jumbo shrimp
¼ cup lemon juice
Dash salt and powdered ginger
1 teaspoon curry powder
2 cans (4 oz. size) shredded coconut
3 cups sifted all-purpose flour
3 teaspoons baking powder
1 teaspoon salt
Few drops yellow food coloring
1 cup milk
Corn oil or sesame oil for deep frying
2 cups curry-flavored cream sauce

Shell shrimp but leave tail intact. Split the back of the shrimp, but do not cut all the way through. Mix lemon juice, salt, ginger, and curry powder; spread over shrimp and marinate for 5 hours. Sprinkle coconut on a tray and bake in a 250° oven until dry. Mix flour, baking powder and salt. Stir in food coloring and milk. Mix to a smooth, thick batter.

Drain shrimp, coat with flour, dip into batter and roll in coconut. Fry in deep hot fat—thermometer should register 375°—until batter is golden. Serve with heated curry sauce.

MEAT BALLS PAPRIKASH

About 20 meat balls

1 pound ground beef, preferably chuck
2 tablespoons grated onion
1 small egg, lightly beaten
2 tablespoons breadcrumbs
Salt and pepper
2 tablespoons butter
2 tablespoons minced onion
1 tablespoon sweet paprika
2 teaspoons caraway seeds, crushed
¾ cup tomato juice
½ clove garlic
1 tablespoon flour
½ cup sour cream

Combine ground beef, grated onion, beaten egg, breadcrumbs, salt and pepper and mix well. Shape into meatballs about 1″ in diameter. Melt butter and slowly saute minced onion until it is soft and pale yellow. Add paprika and crushed caraway seeds and saute for a minute or two over low flame. Add tomato juice and garlic and simmer for 3 or 4 minutes. Turn meat balls into sauce, cover and simmer for about 25 minutes. Twenty minutes before serving, blend flour into sour cream and stir into sauce and heat.

CHICKEN LIVERS CANTONESE

2 *pounds chicken livers*
4 *tablespoons corn oil*
1 *clove garlic, peeled and crushed*
4 *large green peppers, seeded and cut into*
    strips or squares
6 *slices canned pineapple, cut into squares*
2 *cups chicken broth or bouillon*
6 *tablespoons cornstarch*
1 *tablespoon soya sauce*
½ *cup cider vinegar*
½ *cup sugar*
Salt and pepper, to taste

Cut each liver in half and sprinkle with salt and pepper. Heat oil and when it begins to smoke, add livers. Saute until brown on all sides.

Add garlic, green peppers and pineapple and toss in fat until pineapple begins to brown and peppers soften. Remove garlic, add ⅔ cup broth, cover and simmer for 2 or 3 minutes.

Blend cornstarch into soya sauce and add vinegar, sugar, and broth. Pour over vegetables in pan and simmer gently for 5 minutes. Add chicken livers to sauce and heat through.

III

Dips, Spreads, & Patés

CHICKEN LIVER PATE WITH PISTACHIO NUTS

4 to 6 servings

1½ cups chicken broth
2 stalks celery with leaves
1 small onion
6 peppercorns
1 pound chicken livers
½ teaspoon salt
Dash of pepper
2 tablespoons grated onion
2 tablespoons sherry or brandy
2 tablespoons minced, unsalted, shelled
    pistachio nuts
½ cup sweet butter

Simmer the broth with the celery, onion and peppercorns for five minutes; add chicken livers and cook for 10-12 minutes. Remove the livers with a slotted spoon, drain, and grind through fine blade of food chopper. Add all seasonings, sherry, and nuts; toss together and mash in the softened butter, starting with ¼ cup and adding a little at a time until the liver is as smooth as you like it. Pack into a half-pint crock or ramekin, cover with foil or lid, and chill for at least 5 or 6 hours before serving, though overnight would be better. Pate can be spread onto toast directly from the crock, or it can be turned out on a plate and sliced.

EGGPLANT CAVIAR

3 cups

3 large or 4 medium eggplants
4 medium onions, finely minced, or one bunch
*   of scallions, minced tops and all*
1 cup of olive oil
1 cup tomato puree
Juice of two lemons
Salt and pepper, to taste

Boil the eggplant whole for 20 to 30 minutes. Drain, cool, and peel. Chop meat very fine. Saute onion in a little of the oil until it becomes transparent and golden; add eggplant, tomato puree and about a third of the remaining olive oil and cook over low heat for 10 minutes, stirring with a wooden spoon. Add oil gradually as mixture cooks until it is thick and smooth. The mixture should simmer slowly for about 1 hour. Add lemon juice and salt and pepper to taste. Pour into serving dish and chill thoroughly. Sprinkle chopped parsley or chives on top.

FRENCH COUNTRY PATE

About 10 servings

1 pound calves' liver
1¼ pounds country pork sausage meat
½ pound cooked ham
½ pound cooked smoked tongue
1 small onion
1 small clove garlic
½ teaspoon freshly ground black pepper
1 teaspoon salt
Pinch of thyme
1 tablespoon minced parsley
1 tablespoon cognac
5 slices bacon
2 or 3 bay leaves

Remove all sinews and tubes from liver. Using the fine blade of your meat chopper, grind together calves' liver, sausage meat, ham, tongue, onion and garlic. Season with salt, pepper, thyme, parsley and cognac and mix thoroughly, preferably with your hands.

Butter a loaf pan and line with bacon slices. Fill pan with meat mixture and lay bay leaves on top. Cover with buttered paper and set loaf pan into a larger pan that is half-filled with water. Bake in 350° oven for about 1½ hours.

Pate is done when it shrinks from sides of pan and no moisture bubbles out of it.

Remove buttered paper and bay leaves. Cover meat loaf with a cloth and weight it down. Chill overnight. To serve, turn meat out of mold and slice. Garnish with French gherkins; serve with Dijon mustard and French bread.

CHICKPEA AND SESAME DIP

About 1 cup

1 can chickpeas, drained
½ cup canned sesame paste
4 tablespoons lemon juice
1 clove garlic, crushed
Salt
Sesame oil
Parsley

Puree chickpeas in a food mill or blender. Stir or blend in sesame paste, lemon juice, and garlic. Gradually pour in enough oil to give the mixture the consistency of a thick hollandaise sauce. Pour into serving dish. (Sesame oil and paste can be purchased at all health-food stores, or Armenian markets.)

TAPENADE

This tangy vegetable puree is a specialty of the Provence region of France. It can be served with hard-cooked eggs, or it can be used as a spread on toasted French bread. It is also a good filling for celery stalks or cherry tomatoes.

30 salty black Mediterranean olives (These come in cans and can also be found fresh in Italian delicatessens and Greek food shops.)
10 anchovy filets
1½ tablespoons capers
3½ ounces tuna fish (one small can or ½ of a regular can)
½ cup olive oil, approximately
Lemon juice

Remove pits from olives and cut olives into small pieces. Puree olives, anchovies, capers, and tuna fish together, using either a mortar and pestle or a blender at medium speed. As you make the puree, slowly trickle in olive oil and lemon juice alternately, as you would in making mayonnaise. They should be incorporated into the mixture as they are added, so that you finally have a thick, spreadable paste.

Tapenade is traditionally served spread over and spooned around hard-cooked eggs, cut in half lengthwise. You can also mix some of the Tapenade with the mashed egg yolks and then fill the whites with that mixture. Additional sauce can be spooned around the stuffed eggs.

This mixture keeps well in a refrigerator for a week or two. To store, pack into a crock or narrow jar and pour a one-inch layer of olive oil on top to keep air out. Cover. To serve, pour off oil and let mixture stand at room temperature for an hour or two before serving.

VARIATIONS: A tablespoonful of powdered mustard can be added while the mixture is being blended. A few drops of brandy are often added with the olive oil and lemon juice.

¾ pound cream cheese
¾ pound pot cheese
8 anchovy filets, mashed to a fine paste
2 to 3 tablespoons capers
2 tablespoons caraway seeds
3 tablespoons grated onion
2 tablespoons prepared mustard
2 tablespoons paprika
¼ cup flat beer
Salt, to taste
2 cloves garlic

Let cream cheese soften at room temperature. for about 20 minutes.

Cream cheeses together or mix them in a blender until they are smooth and well mixed. With a mortar and pestle, pound anchovies, capers and caraway seeds to a paste and add them to the cheese. Add other ingredients except the garlic and salt. When mixture is smooth and well blended, taste, and salt as needed. Pack into a large crock which you have rubbed with the cut garlic cloves and chill overnight. Serve with pumpernickel squares.

AVOCADO BACON DIP

2½ to 3 cups

6 ounces cream cheese
4 slices bacon, fried and minced
1 large ripe avocado
2 tablespoons lemon juice, or as needed
1 tablespoon grated onion
2 tablespoons olive oil, or as needed
Salt and pepper, to taste
1 clove garlic

Let cream cheese soften for 15 to 20 minutes at room temperature.

Peel avocado, remove pit, and mash, adding 2 tablespoons lemon juice as you do so. Blend cream cheese, onion and bacon into avocado mixture and, drop by drop, add enough olive oil to make the mixture of the correct consistency for dipping. Season to taste.

Rub sides and bottom of serving bowl with a cut clove of garlic. Turn mixture into bowl and chill thoroughly. This dip is especially good with corn chip wafers or raw vegetables such as strips of green pepper, scallions or cucumbers.

If you find the color of this mixture a little drab, a few drops of green food coloring, added before chilling, will brighten it.

BLEU CHEESE AND CHIVE MOUSSE

2 egg yolks
6 tablespoons sweet cream
1 tablespoon finely minced chives
2 tablespoons unflavored gelatin
5 tablespoons cold water
¾ pound Bleu cheese, rubbed through a sieve
1½ cups heavy sweet cream, whipped
3 egg whites, stiffly beaten
Oil, for mold

Beat egg yolks with a fork until frothy. Add cream and stir together. Set over lower part of double boiler half-filled with water. Water in lower part of double boiler should not come to a boil, nor should it touch bottom of upper pan. Cook slowly, stirring almost constantly until mixture is creamy. Add chives.

Soften gelatin in cold water, then set bowl in hot water until gelatin has melted. Stir into hot egg-cream-chive mixture. Add sieved Bleu cheese to mixture, stir through, and cool.

Fold in whipped cream and stiffly beaten egg whites, using a rubber spatula. Fold thoroughly but gently. Wipe a high round 3 cup mold with any unflavored cooking oil. Turn mousse into mold and chill in the refrigerator for 4 hours.

To unmold, dip underside of mold into hot water very quickly, dry and turn over onto serving plate. Garnish with a sprinkling of chives.

POTTED SHRIMP

4 to 6 servings

1 pound shrimp
¼-½ teaspoon mace
Salt and cayenne pepper, to taste
6 tablespoons butter, melted

Cook shrimp for 10-12 minutes in salted water to cover. Drain, cool, peel, devein, chop coarsely and sprinkle with salt, mace and cayenne pepper. Add to 4 tablespoons melted butter in an 8″ skillet and stir with wooden spoon over low flame until butter is absorbed. Taste to correct seasonings. The mixture should be fairly spicy.

Pack firmly into two ramekins or one half-pint crock and pour additional melted butter over the top. It should form a ¼″ layer. If it does not, melt additional butter and pour it on. Cover crock and refrigerate, preferably overnight, but no less than 6 hours before serving. Turn out of molds onto plate and serve with a fork, or if you use a large crock, slice the potted shrimp before serving.

BAGNA CAUDA

Literally translated from the Italian, this dip is a "hot bath," a somewhat inelegant name for an extremely delicious accompaniment to chilled raw vegetables. Serve with strips of carrot, celery, green pepper, fennel, cucumber, scallions, radishes and flowerets of cauliflower and broccoli, as well as raw mushroom caps.

1½ cups

SAUCE:
¾ cup butter
½ cup olive oil
4 cloves garlic, minced
1 small can anchovy filets
1 tablespoon capers, drained and minced
Dash of lemon juice

Heat butter, olive oil and garlic in the top of a double boiler, set over lower pan filled with hot water. Stir constantly during heating so butter and olive oil combine. When butter is melted, remove from heat and stir in anchovies and capers. Finish with a dash of lemon juice. Let stand for 15 minutes. Serve in something that can be set over a warmer.

IV

Canapes, Hot & Cold

Strictly speaking, a canape is based on some sort of cracker, wafer, bread, or toast. Actually, the term also describes a number of small appetizers that are easily handled with the fingers and which can be served from the canape tray. You will find a number of candidates for your canape selection elsewhere in this book, including such things as the Mortadella or Baloney Pie, Deviled Eggs, Beef Tartar Appetizer, the various Cornucopias, Stuffed Cucumber Slices, Smoked Fish Canapes, and many others.

The same is true of hot canapes, which would certainly include such things as Piroshki, Hot Crabmeat Puffs, and so forth.

Flavored butters go a long way in adding to the taste of your canapes. Get into the habit of preparing them—they are simple to make. Let butter soften slightly, then mash and blend with various foods and flavorings that suit the toppings you will use. Some of the things to blend into your butter include minced lobster meat or lobster roe, flaked crabmeat or shrimp, anchovy paste, tuna fish, all sorts of fresh and dried green herbs, curry powder, horseradish, pounded almonds, grated onion, crushed garlic, grated cheese, tomato paste, pimento or even caviar. If you have a blender, use it at high speed to prepare these butters.

In addition to breads and crackers, other good and unusual bases for canapes include cucumber and raw zucchini slices, raw mushroom caps and tiny cherry tomatoes which can be hollowed out and filled with many of the spreads described throughout this book.

Naturally, you will vary your canape selection in shape, color, texture and flavor of topping and garnish. For unusual and decorative shapes, buy a set of canape cutters. The following is only a short list of canape suggestions that should inspire you to dozens more:

1. Spread finger slices of Westphalian pumpernickel or rounds of salty rye bread with lemon-flavored butter and top with shrimp, crabmeat or lobster salad. Decorate with chopped olives or pimento.

2. Spread rounds of Westphalian pumpernickel with chive butter and top with two anchovy filets and a sprinkling of chopped hard-cooked eggs and capers.

3. Spread a round of rye bread with shrimp or lobster butter, top with a whole, peeled, cooked shrimp and a dab of red caviar.

4. Spread a square of Westphalian pumpernickel with horseradish butter. Top with a

cornucopia of smoked salmon filled with a dab of sour cream and dressed with a sprig of dill.

5. Spread a Scandinavian rye wafer with cayenne butter and top with a mixture of minced ham, tongue, and hard-cooked egg bound with mustard-flavored mayonnaise.

6. Spread a finger slice of Westphalian pumpernickel with curry-flavored butter. Top with a small piece of filet of smoked eel and finish with a tiny, paper-thin slice of lemon with the rind cut off.

7. Spread a Scandinavian rye wafer with mustard butter and top with slices of caraway cheese, ham and thin slices of red radish.

8. Spread a square of white bread with horseradish or mustard-flavored butter. Top with thin slices of rare roast beef and finish with some crisply fried, thin onion shreds and crumbled crisp bacon.

9. Cut thin rounds of small French bread and saute in butter or olive oil until golden brown on both sides. Top with Tapenade, Page 46, and slices of hard-cooked egg.

10. Toast white bread, cut in square or finger slices and spread with lemon-flavored butter. Top with finely chopped chicken salad and slivered toasted almonds.

CROSTINI OF CHICKEN LIVERS

About 6 servings

1 pound chicken livers
4 tablespoons minced onion
2 tablespoons butter
⅓ cup chicken stock
½ teaspoon salt
2 teaspoons capers, drained and chopped
6 to 12 rounds of Italian or French bread
Butter or olive oil

Clean livers, remove all connective tissues and chop very fine. Saute onions in butter until soft and yellow. Do not let onions brown. Add chicken stock and simmer for about 3 minutes, or until it has almost evaporated. Add salt and chicken livers. Stir and cook over medium heat until livers turn color and the mixture is fairly firm. Remove from heat and stir in capers. Chill thoroughly in covered jar or bowl.

Fry bread in butter or olive oil until each slice is golden brown on each side. Spread each slice with chicken liver mixture and serve.

MINIATURE PISSALADIERE

This recipe is a standard favorite at the vegetable stalls in the Nice marketplace.

2 to 4 servings

2 English muffins
2 onions, thinly sliced
3 tablespoons olive oil
3 Italian style plum tomatoes, canned
Pinch of dried basil
Salt and pepper, to taste
8 anchovy filets, drained
8 or 10 salty black Italian olives

Split muffins in half and toast lightly on both sides. Set on well-oiled baking sheet or pan.

Heat olive oil. Separate onion slices into rings and simmer very slowly in hot oil. Onions should "melt" and turn bright yellow as they soften. They should be soft in 5 to 8 minutes.

Drain and chop tomatoes and add, with basil, to onions. Simmer uncovered until mixture is dry and tomatoes are blended into onions. Season with salt and pepper.

Spoon onion mixture onto muffin halves. Top each with 2 criss-crossed anchovy filets and dot with halves of olives. Bake in 450° oven for about 15 minutes, or until golden brown.

CROSTINI OF ANCHOVIES

18 to 20 crostini

3 *small cans anchovy filets*
1 *tablespoon grated onion*
1 *clove garlic, crushed*
2 *tablespoons minced parsley*
Pinch of dried oregano
1 *tablespoon capers, drained and chopped*
2 *tablespoons olive oil*
Juice of half a lemon
18 *to 20 small rounds of French or Italian bread*
Butter or olive oil

Mash the anchovies with their oil to a fine paste. Blend in onion, garlic, parsley, oregano, capers, olive oil and lemon juice. Fry bread in butter or olive oil until both sides of each slice are golden brown. Spread one side of each slice with anchovy paste and bake in 475° oven for 5 minutes. Serve hot.

ROQUEFORT CHEESE AND APPLE, AU GRATIN

For each serving

1 thin slice white bread
Butter
1 round slice of peeled apple, ¼" thick
1 slice Roquefort cheese, to cover bread
Paprika

Fry bread slice in a little melted butter, turning once. It should be golden brown on both sides.

Saute apple slice in butter until faintly golden and a little soft—about 3 or 4 minutes on each side. Top bread slice with apple, add cheese, and sprinkle with paprika.

Place under medium flame of broiler until cheese is bubbling and golden brown on top—about 5 or 6 minutes.

Serve on a plate with a knife and fork, or cut in halves so that it can be eaten with the fingers.

RECIPE INDEX

61

Designed by Harald Peter.
Set in Trump Imperial, a Venetian face
designed by Professor Georg Trump
of the Graphic Academy, Munich, Germany.
Printed on Hallmark Eggshell Book paper.